THE WORLD'S GAME

LEARN ALL ABOUT SOCCER

COLORING AND ACTIVITY BOOK

D1309504

RULE 1
COLOR-IT ™

RULE 1
LEARN-IT ™

CREATED BY AL HUBERTS 2012
ILLUSTRATED BY FRANK BAILEY

2 Parents and players show respect for the team, coaches, and officials by arriving on time for practice and games.

KAMAL #9
CENTER FORWARD

COOPER #10
FORWARD RIGHT WING

TREVOR #11
FORWARD LEFT WING

SEAN #12
SUBSTITUTE FULLBACK

LANDON #13
SUBSTITUTE MIDFIELDER

PAULO #14
SUBSTITUTE FORWARD

STEVE
COACH

RENALDO
ASSISTANT COACH

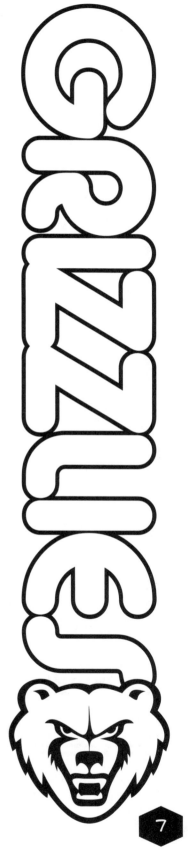

GRIZZLIES

BELLA #1
GOALKEEPER

MEI #2
RIGHT FULLBACK

DAKOTA #3
LEFT FULLBACK

JASMINE #4
RIGHT CENTER BACK

ANNE #5
LEFT CENTER BACK

SOFIE #6
RIGHT MIDFIELDER

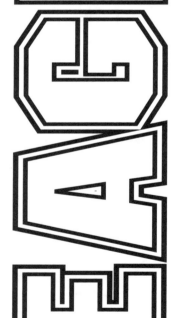

COURTNEY #7
LEFT MIDFIELDER

ASHA #8
CENTER MIDFIELDER

JULIE #9
CENTER FORWARD

EMMA #10
FORWARD RIGHT WING

KARA #11
FORWARD LEFT WING

TAYLOR #12
SUBSTITUTE FORWARD

FATIMA #13
SUBSTITUTE MIDFIELDER

BROOK #14
SUBSTITUTE FULLBACK

ANDREA
COACH

MADISON
ASSISTANT COACH

EAGLES

9

MEGAN #1
GOALKEEPER

KALI #2
RIGHT FULLBACK

AMANDA #3
LEFT FULLBACK

CASSIDY #4
RIGHT CENTER BACK

NIKITA #5
LEFT CENTER BACK

SARAH #6
CENTER MIDFIELDER

LOUISE #7
LEFT MIDFIELDER

McKENZIE #8
RIGHT MIDFIELDER

LILY #9
CENTER FORWARD

JADE #10
FORWARD RIGHT WING

CHLOE #11
FORWARD LEFT WING

TAYLOR #12
SUBSTITUTE FORWARD

ROSE #13
SUBSTITUTE MIDFIELDER

EMILY #14
SUBSTITUTE FULLBACK

CHELSEA
COACH

RACHEL
ASSISTANT COACH

11

JERSEY

SHORTS

SOCKS

SHIN
GUARDS

SOCCER
BOOTS

scoresville bank

COUGARS

COUGARS

All the players on a team wear the same color jersey except the
goalkeepers who wear **different-colored padded jerseys** to distinguish
themselves from their teammates.

A good **soccer boot** will help maximize performance and protect the player from injury.

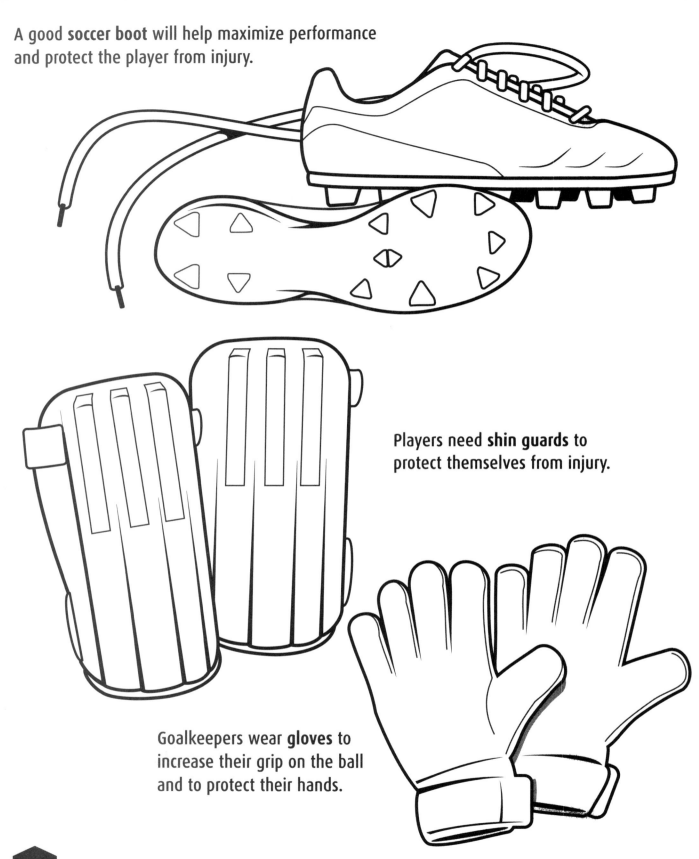

Players need **shin guards** to protect themselves from injury.

Goalkeepers wear **gloves** to increase their grip on the ball and to protect their hands.

14

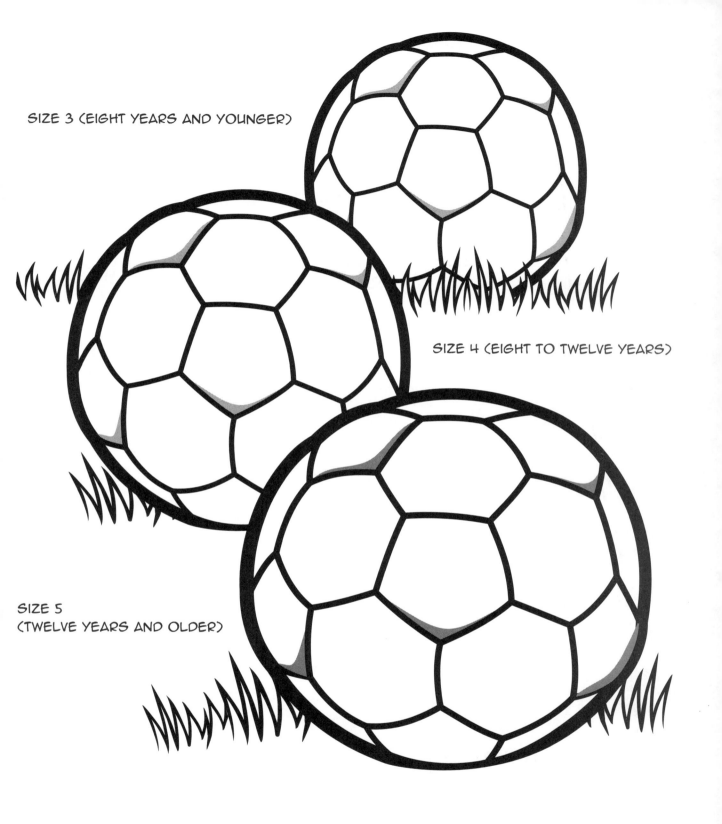

SIZE 3 (EIGHT YEARS AND YOUNGER)

SIZE 4 (EIGHT TO TWELVE YEARS)

SIZE 5
(TWELVE YEARS AND OLDER)

Soccer balls come in different sizes and are made
from **leather** or other suitable material.

15

SOCCER PITCH

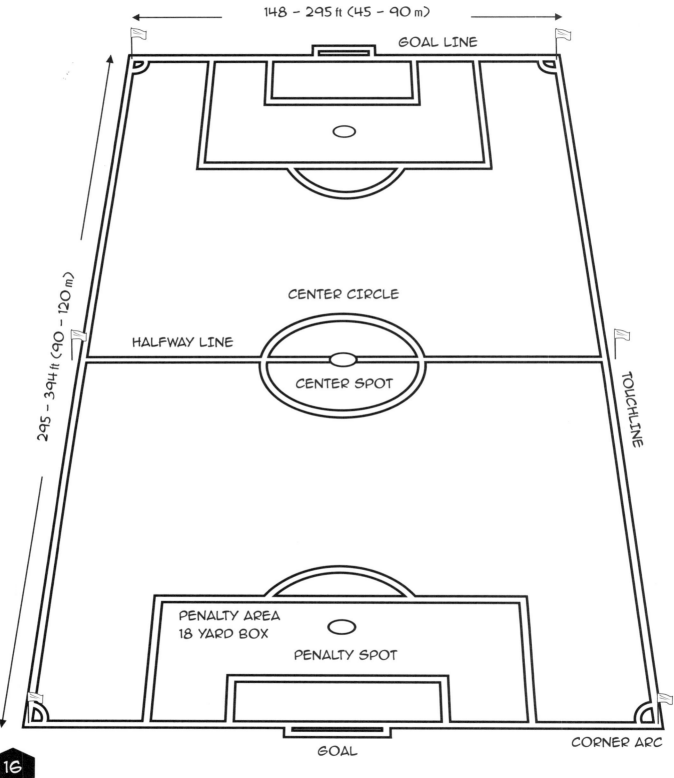

148 – 295 ft (45 – 90 m)

GOAL LINE

295 – 394 ft (90 – 120 m)

CENTER CIRCLE

HALFWAY LINE

CENTER SPOT

TOUCHLINE

PENALTY AREA
18 YARD BOX

PENALTY SPOT

GOAL

CORNER ARC

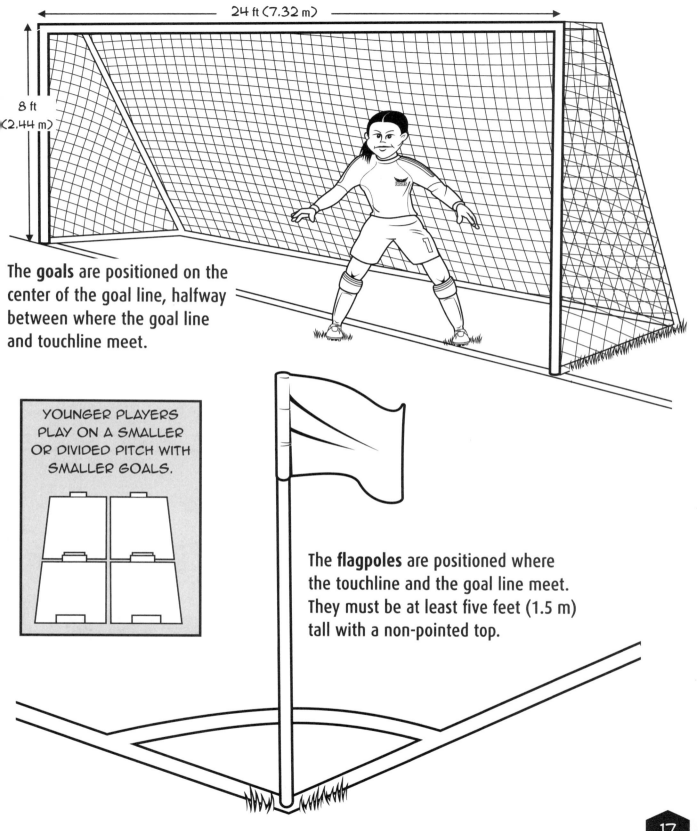

24 ft (7.32 m)

8 ft (2.44 m)

The **goals** are positioned on the center of the goal line, halfway between where the goal line and touchline meet.

YOUNGER PLAYERS PLAY ON A SMALLER OR DIVIDED PITCH WITH SMALLER GOALS.

The **flagpoles** are positioned where the touchline and the goal line meet. They must be at least five feet (1.5 m) tall with a non-pointed top.

GAME OFFICIALS

There is one **referee** who enforces the laws of the game as outlined by FIFA (Fédération Internationale de Football Association). The referee's decisions are final.

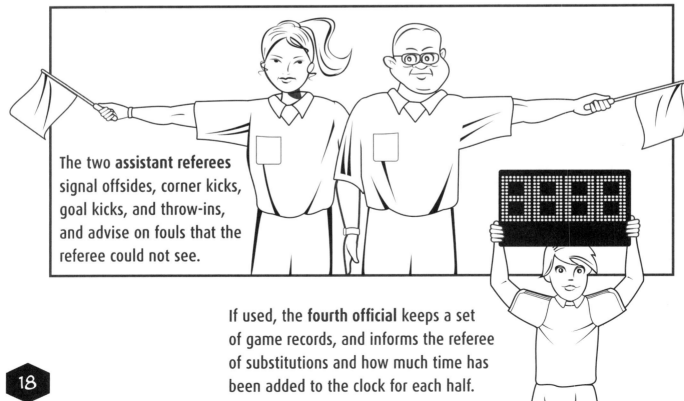

The two **assistant referees** signal offsides, corner kicks, goal kicks, and throw-ins, and advise on fouls that the referee could not see.

If used, the **fourth official** keeps a set of game records, and informs the referee of substitutions and how much time has been added to the clock for each half.

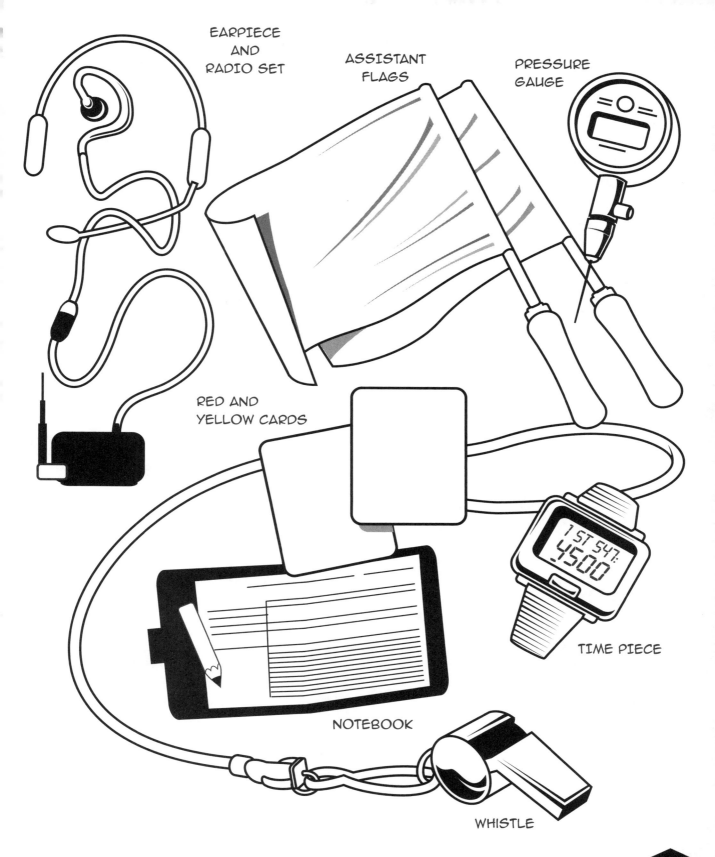

EARPIECE AND RADIO SET

ASSISTANT FLAGS

PRESSURE GAUGE

RED AND YELLOW CARDS

TIME PIECE

1 ST 547:.4500

NOTEBOOK

WHISTLE

Game officials use special equipment.

A soccer game has **two forty-five-minute halves** with a fifteen-minute break between the halves. Younger players may play shorter games.

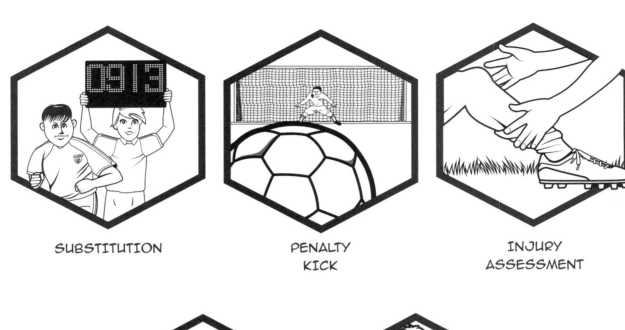

SUBSTITUTION

PENALTY
KICK

INJURY
ASSESSMENT

REMOVAL OF
INJURED PLAYER

WASTED TIME

The referee keeps a record in his notebook of the added time for the reasons shown above.

FINISH

Hotel

START

Can you help the visiting Cougars and Rebels find their way to the stadium?

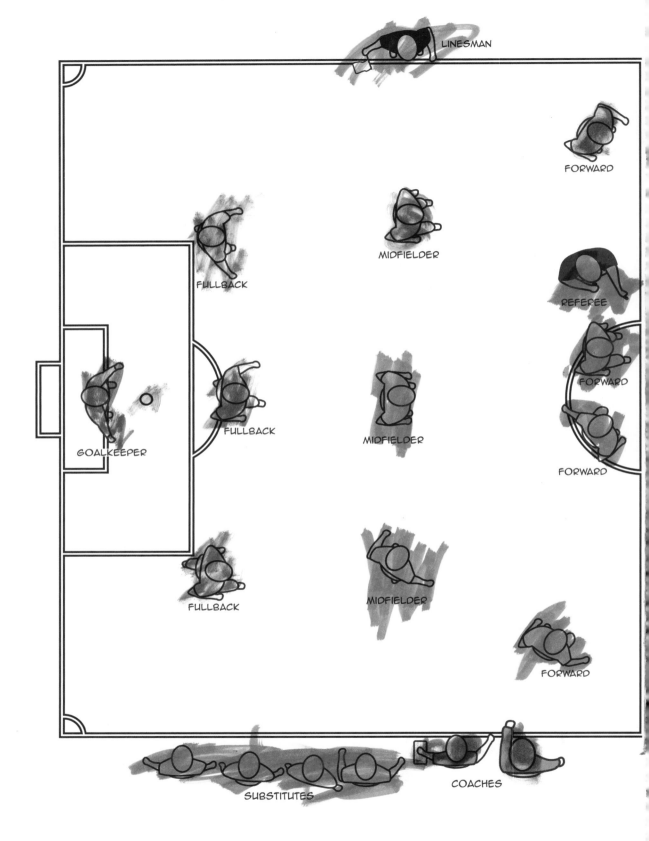

LINESMAN

FORWARD

MIDFIELDER

FULLBACK

REFEREE

FORWARD

FULLBACK

MIDFIELDER

GOALKEEPER

FORWARD

FULLBACK

MIDFIELDER

FORWARD

SUBSTITUTES

COACHES

22

The Eagles and Rebels players are all positioned for the start of the game.
This is a **3-3-4 formation.**

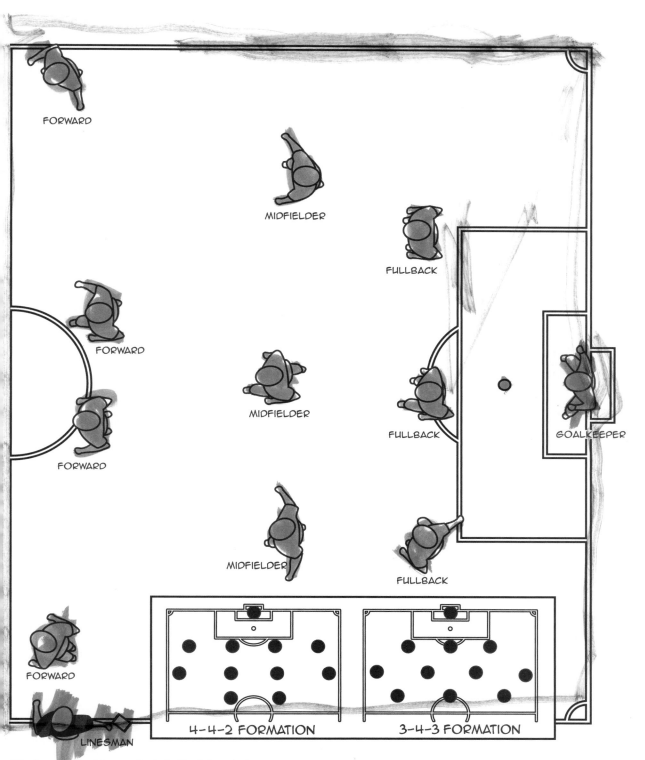

FORWARD

MIDFIELDER

FULLBACK

FORWARD

MIDFIELDER

FULLBACK

GOALKEEPER

FORWARD

MIDFIELDER

FULLBACK

FORWARD

4-4-2 FORMATION

3-4-3 FORMATION

LINESMAN

All players must be on their half of the pitch.

The ball must be stationary on the center mark.

The ball is in play when kicked and moved forward.

Players must wait for the referee's signal to start play.

The opposing team must be 10 yards (9.5 m) from the ball until it is in play.

The kicker must not touch the ball again until it has been touched by another player.

23

Eagles captain Courtney and Rebels captain Lily take part in the coin toss.
The Eagles win the **coin toss** and decide which goal to attack in the first half.
They will attack the **opposite** goal in the second half.

24

MATCH THE DESCRIPTION TO THE CORRECT SOCCER TERM #1

____ ADVANTAGE CLAUSE RULE

____ ASSIST

____ ATTACKING

____ BANANA KICK

____ BICYCLE KICK

____ BREAKAWAY

____ CENTER CIRCLE

____ CENTER BACK

____ CENTER SPOT

____ CHEST TRAP

____ CHIP PASS

____ CHIP SHOT

1. A ball kicked over an opposing player to a teammate.

2. The team member who plays in the center of the defensive line.

3. A ball kicked in midair, backward, over the kicker's head.

4. The circle positioned in the middle of the pitch.

5. A ball kicked over the goalkeeper's head into the goal.

6. What the team in possession of the ball is doing when moving the ball forward.

7. When an attacker with the ball has no defender between themselves and the goal.

8. Rule that allows the referee to not stop play if stopping the play would benefit the team that committed the foul.

9. When a player uses their chest to stop a ball.

10. The spot from where kickoffs are taken to start a game.

11. A kick that curves the ball inward.

12. A pass from a teammate that results in a goal being scored.

WORD SEARCH #1
EQUIPMENT & PITCH REFERENCE

```
C A K C I Y E S R E J S
E R O S Y S N F G C A H
L O O G E L I E L R E I
T O B O L O L D L A U N
S C E A L L H A N R G G
I C T L O G C S B E R U
H U O C W S U A A N W A
W T N S C W O N S R R R
A P E N A L T Y B O X D
T O P S R E T N E C N R
J E R E D C A R D D S G
C R O S S B A R H P O R
```

BALL
CENTER SPOT
CORNER ARC
CROSSBAR
FLAG

GOAL
JERSEY
NOTEBOOK
PENALTY BOX
RED CARD

SHIN GUARD
SHOES
TOUCHLINE
WHISTLE
YELLOW CARD

26

CROSSWORD #1
SOCCER PERSONNEL

ACROSS

2. THE PLAYER WHO LEADS THE TEAM ON THE PITCH
3. A PLAYER WHO TRIES TO STOP THE OPPOSITION FROM SCORING
5. THE TEAM BOSS WHO GUIDES THE TEAM FROM THE SIDELINES
7. THE PERSON WHO MAKES SURE THE RULES OF THE GAME ARE FOLLOWED
8. THE PLAYER WHO PLAYS BEHIND THE TWO CENTER HALVES
9. THEY DECIDE AND SIGNAL IF A BALL IS OUT OF PLAY
12. A PLAYER THAT PLAYS ALONG THE OUTER EDGE OF THE PITCH
13. A PLAYER THAT PLAYS ON THE FRONT LINE
14. THE PLAYER THAT CAN USE THEIR HANDS

DOWN

1. ALSO CALLED A MIDFIELDER
4. A PLAYER WHO IS ON THE PITCH WHEN THE PLAY BEGINS
6. A PLAYER WHO TAKES A PASS FROM A TEAMMATE
8. A PLAYER WHO REPLACES ANOTHER PLAYER
10. A PLAYER WITH THE BALL
11. A FORWARD WHO IS A STRONG GOAL SCORER

Rebels forward Jade knows that kicking a ball against a wall can help her learn how to better **control** it.

Eagles defenders Dakota and Anne know that **passing** the ball while **dribbling**
will help improve their play.

29

30

Grizzlies center back Charlie knows that **juggling** the ball
will help improve his ball handling skills.

Cougars center back Jafar shows how to **receive** and **control** the ball with his **head**, **thigh**, and **chest**.

31

Grizzlies midfielder Aiden uses his chest to **trap** the ball by leaning back and **cushioning** it to reduce its momentum.

Courtney, the Cougars' assistant coach, yells "**Man on!**" to Cougars center back
Jafar to warn him that Grizzlies midfielder Lucas is approaching. Jafar receives the ball
with his **thigh** at a forty-five-degree angle. This helps him to gain control of it.

33

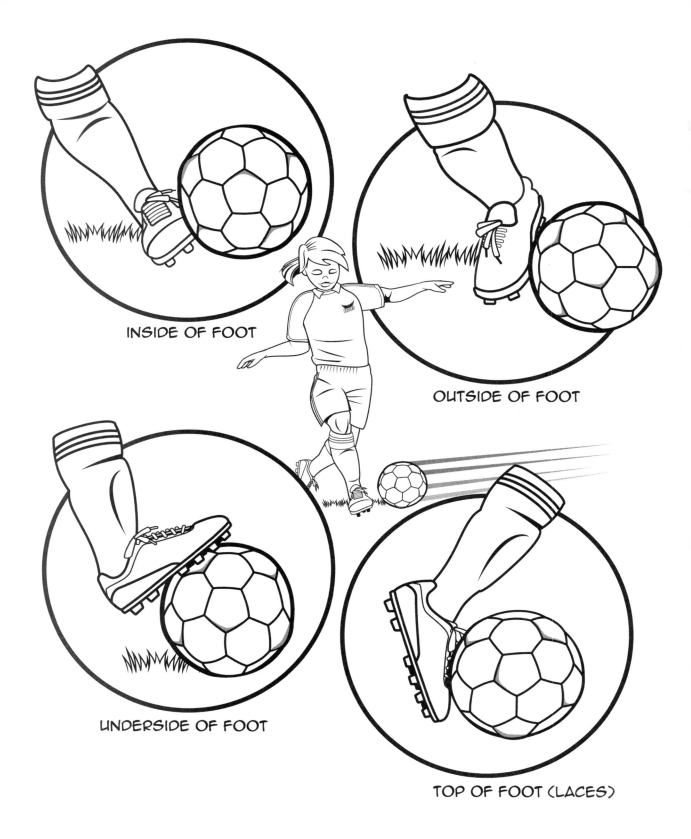

INSIDE OF FOOT

OUTSIDE OF FOOT

UNDERSIDE OF FOOT

TOP OF FOOT (LACES)

 34 Eagles midfielder Sofie uses a **light touch** when receiving the ball to gain control.

Eagles midfielder Sofie uses the **underside** of her foot to gain control of the ball.

Cougars forward Logan receives the ball with his **head** and directs it to the ground to gain control of it.

_____ CHANNELS   _____ CORNER KICK   _____ CUT THE ANGLE

_____ CLEAR THE BALL   _____ CREATING SPACE   _____ DEFENDERS

_____ CORNER ARC   _____ CROSS PASS   _____ DEFENSIVE WALL

_____ CORNER FLAG   _____ CROSSBAR   _____ DEFLECTION

1. The flag located where the touchlines and goal lines meet.

2. A pass by a player near the sideline to a teammate near the middle or opposite side of the field.

3. When the goalkeeper reduces the amount of space the attacker has to shoot on the net.

4. The players on the team not in possession of the ball.

5. Lineup of defending players, pressed shoulder to shoulder, protecting their goal against a free kick.

6. Kick the ball away from the goal area.

7. When a player directs an opposing player away from the play with their body, usually toward the wings.

8. Change in the ball's direction after hitting the goalpost.

9. A restart from the corner arc.

10. The bar on the top of the goal, connecting the two side posts.

11. The quarter circle from where corner kicks must be taken.

12. When attacking players draw opposing players away from a teammate who has the ball.

38

Rebels midfielder Sarah keeps the ball **close to her feet** to avoid a tackle from Eagles midfielder Asha.

1.

2.

3.

Grizzlies forward Kamal surprised Cougars center back Ethan. Rather than passing
the ball to Grizzlies forward Cooper, he performed a **step over** and continued to run.

Rebels midfielder McKenzie dribbles the ball close to her feet, **shielding** it from opposing players to avoid a turnover.

Spot the ten differences between pages 40 and 41.

STEP 1.

STEP 2.

STEP 3.

STEP 4.

Grizzlies midfielder James uses an **inside hook** to avoid
a tackle from Cougars midfielder Jacob.

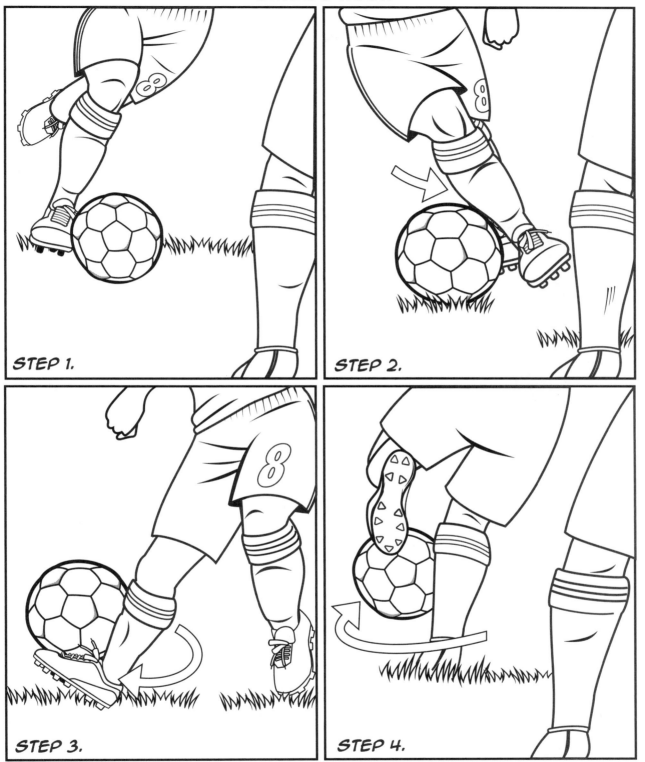

STEP 1.

STEP 2.

STEP 3.

STEP 4.

Cougars midfielder Andrew uses an **outside hook** to avoid a tackle from Grizzlies midfielder Aiden.

Cougars forward Tyler performs a **scissor move** in order to get the ball past Grizzlies fullback Sean.

With **open space**, Cougars midfielder Jacob is able to run fast and control
his dribbling. He does not have to be as concerned about protecting the ball.
It is important that Jacob keep his head up.

45

Eagles forward Emma was fooled by Rebels fullback Kali who only pretended she was going to kick the ball.

Rebels midfielder Sarah stumble[s]
She was fooled by Eagles fullba[ck]
Dakota's **fake** mov[e]

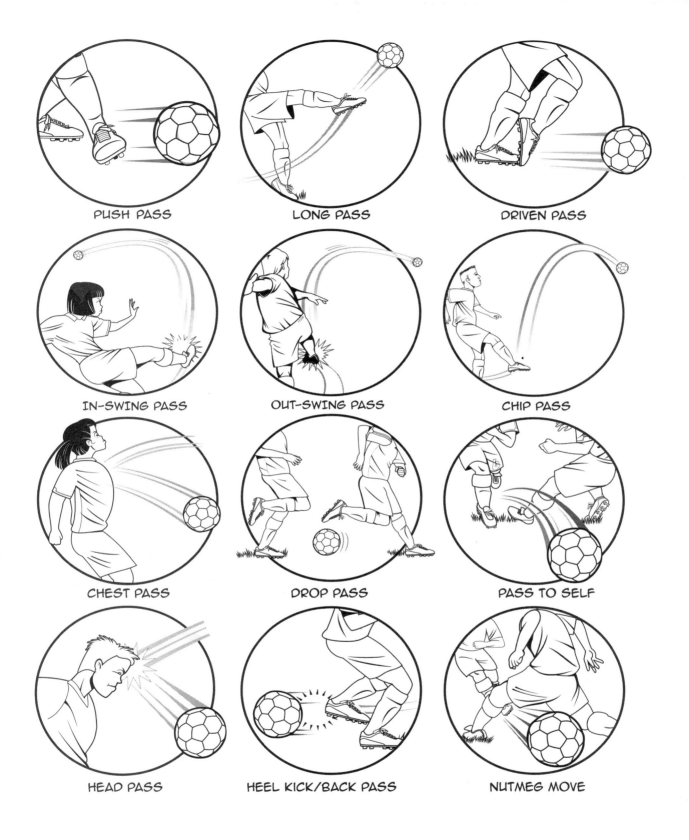

PUSH PASS

LONG PASS

DRIVEN PASS

IN-SWING PASS

OUT-SWING PASS

CHIP PASS

CHEST PASS

DROP PASS

PASS TO SELF

HEAD PASS

HEEL KICK/BACK PASS

NUTMEG MOVE

There are different ways to pass the ball. Players pass the ball to
clear it from danger, to **keep possession**, or to **set up a scoring opportunity**.

47

The **push pass** is the most accurate type of pass.
Push passes are used for shorter distances along the ground.

Players **mark** their opponents by guarding and preventing them from advancing the ball. A **long pass** can be very effective because defenders do not mark opposing players as closely when they are farther away from the ball.

Cougars midfielder Liam makes a **driven pass**. He knows it's always better to pass the ball if a teammate is in a **better position**.

The curve created with an **out-swing** pass makes it more difficult for the opposing players to judge where the ball will land.

Rebels midfielder Louise makes a **back-heel pass**
to avoid a tackle from Eagles fullback Brook.

Grizzlies forward Kamal was **nutmegged**. The ball was passed through his legs.

Cougars forward Kris makes a **chip pass**, giving the ball loft and sending it over Grizzlies fullback Lucas's head.

Eagles midfielder Fatima does a subtle **flick pass** to Eagles forward Kara.

_____ DIRECT FREE KICK   _____ DRILL   _____ FIFA

_____ DIVE   _____ DROP BALL   _____ FLICK HEADER

_____ DRAW   _____ DROPKICK   _____ FORMATIONS

_____ DRIBBLE   _____ FAKE   _____ FOURTH OFFICIAL

1. Fédération Internationale de Football Association, the world governing body of soccer.

2. Exercises a coach takes players through to teach them soccer skills.

3. To pretend to have an injury in an attempt to fool the referee into giving an opposing player a foul.

4. The official who informs the referee of substitutions and time added to the clock.

5. To control the ball with your feet while moving.

6. A move intended to deceive an opposing player.

7. The positioning of players that a team uses. For example, four fullbacks, three halfbacks, and three forwards.

8. A game ending with a tied score.

9. When a goalkeeper drops the ball from their hands and then kicks it just after it hits the ground.

10. A kick awarded to a player for a serious infraction committed by an opposing team member.

11. A method a referee uses to restart play by dropping the ball between two players.

12. Deflection of the ball with a subtle movement of the head.

Grizzlies midfielder James pops the ball into the air in an attempt to pass it to himself. Luckily he is faster than Cougars fullback Daniel!

```
S W E E P E R F N A K R
C I O R E K I R T S E R
K S U B S T I T U T E C
C C W I N I A C R P N O
A D A I S C I A E A R A
B E I B K O T E M S R C
L F A E F S K S O M W H
L E R E D L E I F D I M
U N L E A N A A I M N E
F D E O I E E H E R G R
E E G L R E F E R E E M
D R A W R O F S A A R A
```

ATTACKER
COACH
DEFENDER
FORWARD
FULLBACK

GOALKEEPER
HALFBACK
LINESMAN
MIDFIELDER
REFEREE

STARTER
STRIKER
SUBSTITUTE
SWEEPER
WINGER

MAZE #2
SOCCER BALL

FINISH

START

Can you help Logan find his way from the center of the ball to its outer rim?

Rebels midfielder Rose kicks a **half-volley** over Eagles midfielder Asha to her teammate, midfielder McKenzie.

Grizzlies fullback Lucas kicks a long **full-volley** pass towards Grizzlies forward Paulo.

Rebels goalkeeper Megan **punts** the ball to open space just ahead of her target, Rebels forward Chloe.

Cougars center back Ethan executes a perfect **bicycle kick**.
A player would receive a yellow card if this were done in an unsafe situation.

Grizzlies goalkeeper Garret **drop-kicks** the ball down
the field toward the Grizzlies' midfield.

Players should avoid toe kicks.
They are unpredictable as Eagles center back Jasmine has shown.

WORD SCRAMBLE A-D

USE THE CLUES TO UNSCRAMBLE THE SOCCER WORD

Clue	Scramble	
PLAY ON AFTER FOUL	TAGEVANAD WAL	_____
TO HELP	TISSSA	_____
PLAYER WHO HAS BALL POSSESSION	ACKERATT	_____
UPSIDE-DOWN KICK	ELCYCIB KCIK	_____
TO GET AWAY	WYAAAKERB	_____
PLAYER WHO LEADS THE TEAM ON THE PITCH	NIACPAT	_____
WHERE THE GAME STARTS	REENTC OPTS	_____
RUN INTO ANOTHER PLAYER	HARCEG	_____
WILL SLOW THE BALL	TESHC RAPT	_____
PASS IN THE AIR	IPCH ASSP	_____
THEY GIVE SHOES TRACTION	TEALSC	_____
AT THE CORNERS	RENROC CAR	_____
TYPE OF RESTART	RNEROC ICKK	_____
TOP PART OF GOALPOST	RABROSCS	_____
PLAYERS NOT IN POSSESSION OF THE BALL	DERSFENDE	_____

Eagles fullback Dakota **slide tackles** Rebels forward Jade.

Rebels fullback Emily **poke tackles** the ball from Eagles midfielder Sofie.

Eagles center back Anne **hook tackles** Rebels midfielder Sarah.

Cougars fullback Mason keeps his foot low. This will help get the ball from Grizzlies forward Cooper using a **block tackle**.

Cougars center back Ethan makes a **recovery tackle** on Grizzlies
forward Trevor, stopping his advance on the Cougars' goal.

Eagles fullback Brook makes a legal **shoulder tackle** on Rebels forward Chloe.

A shoulder tackle cannot take place from behind, or be violent or dangerous,
and is only permitted within three feet of the ball.

 The player must have one foot on the ground, be shoulder to shoulder with their
opponent with their arms close to the body, and they must be intending to win the ball.

MATCH THE DESCRIPTION TO THE CORRECT SOCCER TERM #4

_____ 4-3-3	_____ FRONT HEADER	_____ GOALKEEPER
_____ FIRST TOUCH	_____ FULLBACKS	_____ GOAL KICK
_____ FORWARDS	_____ GIVE AND GO	_____ GOAL LINE
_____ FOUL	_____ GOAL AREA	_____ HALFBACK

1. A kick taken to restart the game from inside the goal area, used when the attacking team has kicked the ball past the defending team's goal line.

2. The line that forms the boundary of play at each end of the pitch.

3. A violation of the rules for which the referee awards a free kick.

4. Players who usually score most of a team's goals. They play in front of the rest of the players.

5. A rectangular area in front of each goal.

6. Players whose main responsibility is to prevent the opposing team from scoring.

7. A formation that determines the position of the players.

8. A player's first contact with the ball.

9. The player who can use their hands to handle the ball in the goal area.

10. Players who link the fullbacks and the forwards. Also called midfielders.

11. When a player passes the ball to a teammate then runs past an opposing player to receive the ball back from the teammate.

12. The most common type of header, involving a player hitting the ball with their forehead.

76

The ball is in the air approximately 30 per cent of the time so players must learn to **head** the ball.

Rebels center back Cassidy **flicks** the ball with her head, redirecting it to Rebels midfielder Louise. This ensures that Eagles forward Emma does not gain control.

Eagles forward Julie dives for the ball and uses a **front header** to try to score a goal. Rebels goalkeeper Megan makes an amazing save!

CROSSWORD #2
SOCCER TERMS

CROSS

A PLAYER OR TEAM WHO HAS CONTROL OF THE BALL

A LEGAL TACKLE IF DONE CORRECTLY

COLOR OF THE CARD THAT WARNS PLAYERS OF UNSPORTSMANLIKE BEHAVIOR

PROTECTING THE BALL FROM AN OPPOSING PLAYER WITH ONE'S BODY

KICKING THE BALL TO A TEAMMATE

MOVE BY THE GOALKEEPER TO STOP THE BALL FROM GOING INTO THE NET

PRETENDING TO BE INJURED

A TYPE OF KICK A GOALKEEPER MAKES

A TYPE OF KICK MADE FROM WHERE THE GOAL LINE AND TOUCHLINE INTERSECT

DOWN

2. WHEN A TEAM HAS FEWER PLAYERS THAN THE OPPOSING TEAM

3. A PLAYER KICKS THE BALL BETWEEN AN OPPOSING PLAYER'S LEGS

4. PLAYERS DO BOTH AN INSIDE AND OUTSIDE VERSION OF THIS MOVE

5. FANCY FOOT MOVE TO GET BY AN OPPOSING PLAYER

8. WHEN A TEAM CALLS FOR AN OFFICIAL BREAK IN PLAY

10. WHAT A PLAYER DOES TO GET THE BALL FROM AN OPPOSING PLAYER

SOCCER DRILLS

Pass Possession drills teach players to maintain possession of the ball while moving quickly in a small space.

The **Dribble Around the Cone** and **Pass Relay drills** teach players to run with the ball, how to make and receive passes at game speed, one-touch control, and how to pass in open space.

80

The **Keep Away passing game** teaches the attacker to control and
pass the ball, and it teaches defenders to challenge for the ball.

The **Dribble Across a Square game** teaches players control and speed dribbling, how to look up and dribble through traffic, and how to shield the ball.

With the **50/50 drill**, players work on their fitness, winning 50/50 balls, shooting, and goalkeeping.

THROW-IN

Eagles center back Jasmine delivers a perfect **throw-in** to her teammate, midfielder Sofie.
Jasmine knows she cannot touch the ball until another player does so first.
The throw-in is taken from where the ball crossed the touchline.

NO REBELS

THROW-IN

Spot the ten differences between pages 84 and 85.

Throw-ins are an important part of the game.

Tips for throw-ins:

- Avoid side spin.
- Drag the toes of your rear foot.
- Hold the ball behind your head, elbows out.
- Remain upright, follow through, and snap your wrists.
- Throw the ball high (as if going over an opponent's head).

_____ HALFTIME   _____ HOOK   _____ IN-SWING PASS

_____ HALF VOLLEY   _____ IN BOUNDS   _____ JUGGLING

_____ HANDBALL   _____ INDIRECT FREE KICK _____ KICKOFF

_____ HAT TRICK   _____ IN PLAY   _____ LINESMEN

1. When the ball is inside the boundaries of the field and the referee has not stopped play.

2. To kick the ball while it is still in the air after it has bounced once.

3. How a game is started or restarted after a goal.

4. The intermission between the two halves of the game.

5. A pass that curves inward, while in flight, like a banana.

6. The officials who assist the referee.

7. Describes the ball when it is inside the touchlines and goal lines.

8. A type of tackle used to get the ball from an opposing player.

9. A kick awarded for a less serious foul.

10. Keeping the ball in the air without the use of your hands.

11. When a player scores three goals in a single game.

12. Touching the ball with a hand or arm.

GO EAGLES

Direct free kicks are awarded if a player
- holds, pushes, charges, or jumps at an opposing player;
- deliberately handles the ball;
- spits, trips, kicks, strikes, or attempts any of these actions against an opposing player or official;
- when tackling to gain control of the ball, makes contact with an opposing player prior to touching the ball.

DIRECT FREE KICK

88

DIRECT FREE KICK

Direct free kicks are taken from the spot where the offense occurred.
If a direct free kick goes into a team's own goal, a corner kick is awarded.
The defending team forms a defensive wall to try and block the ball.

PENALTY

A direct free kick infraction in the penalty area results in a **penalty kick**.
No other players are allowed in their penalty area until the ball is in motion.
A goal may be scored directly from a penalty kick.

GOAL KICK

Eagles forward Emma kicked the ball past the Rebels' goal line but not into the goal.
The Rebels are awarded a **goal kick**.

INDIRECT FREE KICK

Indirect free kicks are awarded to the opposing team if a **player**

- plays in a dangerous manner;
- impedes the progress of an opposing player;
- prevents the goalkeeper from releasing the ba[ll] from his hands; or
- commits any offense for which play is stoppe[d] caution or send the player off the pitch.

Indirect free kicks are also awarded if a **goalkee[per]**

- holds the ball for more than six seconds;
- touches the ball after releasing it before anoth[er] player touches it;
- touches the ball if it was deliberately kicked t[o] him by a teammate; or
- touches the ball with their hands if it was directly received from a throw-in.

The referee awards an indirect free kick to the Eagles. On the kickoff,
Rebels forward Lily **touched the ball twice** before it was touched by another player.

INDIRECT FREE KICK

INDIRECT FREE KICK

On an indirect free kick, the ball must be **touched by a second player** before a goal can be scored. It is taken from where the offense occurred unless it was committed in the goal area of the team awarded the kick. In this case, the kick can be taken from anywhere in the goal area. An indirect free kick within the opposition's goal area is taken from the line parallel to the goal line.

94

INDIRECT FREE KICK

The Eagles are awarded an indirect free kick. Rebels goalkeeper Megan **handled the ball** that was deliberately kicked to her teammate, fullback Emily.

95

GOAL KICK

A **goal kick** is awarded when the ball passes over the goal line (not into the goal) and was last touched by a player from the attacking team. The opposing team must stay out of the penalty area until the ball is in play (when it is kicked out of the penalty area). The ball is kicked from any poi in the goal area and must be touched by another player before it can be touched by the kicker agai

A **corner kick** is awarded when the ball passes over the goal line (not into the goal)
and was last touched by a player from the defending team. The ball is placed in the corner
arc closest to where the ball crossed the goal line and is in play once it has been kicked.
The ball must be touched by another player before the kicker can touch it again.

97

GOAL

Grizzlies forward Paulo takes a corner kick and scores a goal. Goalies must be aware of players in the **danger zone**. The danger zone is the area in front of the goal from where it would be easiest to score a goal.

The Grizzlies scored a goal. Cougars center forward Kris
takes a **kickoff** at the center spot to restart the game.
Kickoffs are taken
    at the start of the game, each extra period, and the second half;
    after a goal has been scored.

99

WORD SCRAMBLE D-O

USE THE CLUES TO UNSCRAMBLE THE SOCCER WORD

CHANGE OF DIRECTION   TIONFLECDE   _____

MOVING THE BALL   BLINGDRIB   _____

TYPE OF RESTART   OPRD ALLB   _____

TO FOOL   KEAF   _____

UP FRONT   FWARDOR INLE   _____

GIVEN IF A FOUL OCCURS   REFE ICKK   _____

LAST DEFENDER   LAOGEPEREK   _____

TIME TO REST   ALFHEMIT   _____

TOUCHING BALL WITH ILLEGAL BODYPART   NDAHLABL   _____

LET'S GET STARTED   KOFKIFC   _____

SENT AHEAD   DEAL SAPS   _____

THEY WATCH THE LINES   ESMNELIN   _____

STAY ON YOUR MARK   ANM-OT-MNA   _____

WORKS THE MIDDLE   ELDERIFDIM   _____

IN CONTROL   ICFFOIALS   _____

A **dropped ball** is used to restart the game after a temporary stoppage while the ball is in play. A dropped ball cannot be kicked until it has touched the ground.

101

FOUL BY ATTACKER

Cougars forward Logan receives a yellow card for **unsportsmanlike behavior.**
He faked an injury.

FOUL BY ATTACKER

Spot the ten differences between pages 102 and 103.

FOUL BY DEFENDER

104

Cougars fullback Mateo receives a yellow card for **holding** Grizzlies midfielder James, preventing him from getting the ball. A **yellow card** warns a player of dangerous or unsportsmanlike behavior, or for breaking the rules of the game.

FOUL BY DEFENDER

Rebels center back Nikita receives a yellow card. She is **positioned too close** to Eagles midfielder Asha as she takes a throw-in.

FOUL BY ATTACKER

Grizzlies forward Trevor receives a yellow card for **delaying the restart of play**.

FOUL BY ATTACKER

Cougars forward Kris receives a yellow card for preventing the Grizzlies' goalkeeper from putting the ball back in play.

Eagles fullback Mei receives a yellow card for **leaving the pitch**.
She did not have permission from the referee.

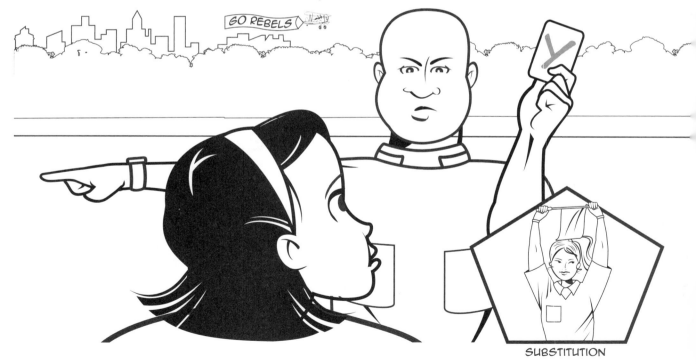

SUBSTITUTION

108

Eagles forward Taylor receives a yellow card and must leave the pitch.
She did not have permission from the referee to enter the pitch as a substitution.

FOUL BY DEFENDER

Cougars midfielder Andrew is called for **impeding the progress** of an opposing player. He blocked Grizzlies forward Cooper from getting to the ball before it crossed the touchline. This is unsportsmanlike behavior.

109

FOUL BY ATTACKER

Grizzlies fullback Lucas receives a yellow card for **distracting an opposing player.** Because Lucas has received two yellow cards, he also receives a red card and must leave the pitch.

FOUL BY ATTACKER

Grizzlies forward Trevor receives a yellow card.
He **gained an advantage** by leaning on his teammate.

FOUL BY DEFENDER

Rebels fullback Kali receives a yellow card.
Players cannot show **dissent toward referees**.

FOUL BY DEFENDER

112 Grizzlies forward Paulo and midfielder Landon receive yellow cards for **sandwiching** Cougars midfielder Andrew, stopping him from getting back into the play.

WORD SCRAMBLE O-S

USE THE CLUES TO UNSCRAMBLE THE SOCCER WORD

OUT OF POSITION	FSIFODE	_____
IN THE CLEAR	ENPO	_____
AFTER NINETY MINUTES	OVEREMIT	_____
MOVING THE BALL	ASSPGIN	_____
GOALKEEPER STOPS THE BALL	VEAS	_____
TYPE OF SHOT	LTYENAP OTSH	_____
FIELD OF PLAY	ITCHP	_____
TO HAVE CONTROL OF THE BALL	SSSSEIONPO	_____
WAY OF MOVING THE BALL	SHUP SASP	_____
PLAYER WHO GETS THE BALL	ERVIECER	_____
REQUIRED TO LEAVE GAME	EDR RACD	_____
PITCH BOSS	EEREREF	_____
GET A POINT	CORES	_____
PROTECTING THE BALL	INGSHIDLE	_____
LEG PROTECTION	GUARSDNIH	_____

113

ADVANTAGE

Grizzlies forward Cooper has a good opportunity to score so the referee uses the **advantage clause rule.** This allows play to continue despite Cougars center back Ethan tripping Grizzlies forward Kamal.

FOUL BY DEFENDER

Grizzlies fullback Sean receives a **red card**. He **deliberately used his hands** to stop the ball from going into the goal. The Cougars are awarded the goal.

115

FOUL BY DEFENDER

116 **Grizzlies midfielder Joel receives a red card for holding Cougars midfielder Andrew.** Andrew had an obvious breakaway and scoring opportunity.

FOUL BY ATTACKER

Rebels fullback Emily receives a red card for
deliberately using **excess force** when tackling Eagles fullback Dakota.

117

_____ LAWS OF THE GAME   _____ MLS   _____ OFFENSIVE PLAYERS

_____ LOFT   _____ MIDFIELD LINE   _____ OFFICIALS

_____ MAN ON   _____ NET   _____ OFFSIDE

_____ MARK   _____ NUTMEG   _____ ONSIDE

1. An arching kick that sends the ball high into the air.

2. To pass the ball through an opposing player's legs.

3. A warning to a teammate that a player from the opposing team is close by.

4. The referee and linesmen.

5. To guard an opposing player, preventing them from advancing the ball.

6. Describes a player who is positioned to receive the ball and is not offside.

7. The line that divides the playing field in half.

8. Players on the team that has the ball.

9. Describes an attacking player who is positioned ahead of both the ball and the last defender, and is part of the play.

10. The material attached to the goalposts and crossbar; it stops the ball.

11. The official FIFA term used to describe the rules of soccer.

12. North America's premier soccer league.

WORD SEARCH #3
PLAY TERMS

```
S P V O P A K N D B A
R K C I K R E N R O C
F I H F C V W E A D D
C C A S I I A P W L D
A K R D K K I O E F F
E O G O A L P O S T W
A F E W N J A F C S O
B F A A A S S I S T O
A Y C G N I L G G U J
R Y L L A B P O R D L
B A L A B F E N O K O
```

ASSIST

BANANA KICK

BREAKAWAY

CHARGE

CHIP

CORNER KICK

DIVE

DRAW

DROP BALL

FAKE

FLANK

GOALPOST

JUGGLING

KICKOFF

OPEN

IN PLAY

DEFLECTION OFF THE GOALPOST

DEFLECTION OFF THE FLAG POST

REBOUND OFF THE LINESMAN OR REFEREE

POSITIONS OF THE BALL ALONG BUT NOT OVER THE TOUCHLINE

PITCH

OUT OF PLAY

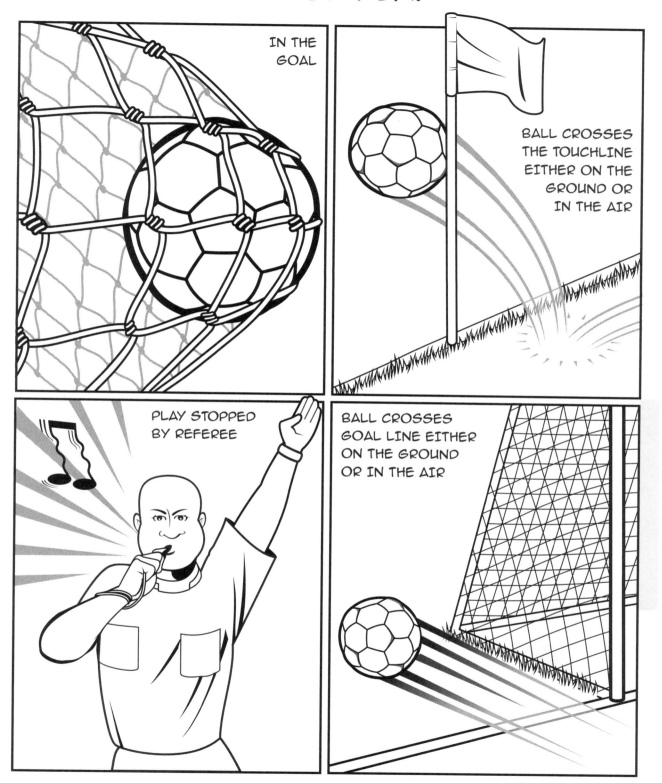

Cougars forward Logan is **offside.** He is positioned ahead of the ball
and the Grizzlies' last defender, fullback Sean.

In this picture, Logan is **onside.**
He is even with the Grizzlies' last defender, fullback Sean.

GOAL KICK

THROW-IN

CORNER KICK

There is no offside if the player receives the ball from a
goal kick, throw-in, or corner kick.

MAZE #3
FIELD OF PLAY

START

GOOAALL!!!

124

Can you help Eagles midfielder Asha dribble the
ball from her goal line to the Rebels' goal?

REFEREE SIGNAL GAME
MATCH THE REFEREE OR
LINESMAN TO THE CORRECT SIGNAL

◯ ADVANTAGE ◯ DIRECT FREE KICK ◯ GOAL ◯ SENDING OFF
◯ CAUTION ◯ FOUL BY ATTACKER ◯ INDIRECT FREE KICK ◯ SUBSTITUTION
◯ CORNER KICK ◯ FOUL BY DEFENDER ◯ OFFSIDE ◯ THROW-IN

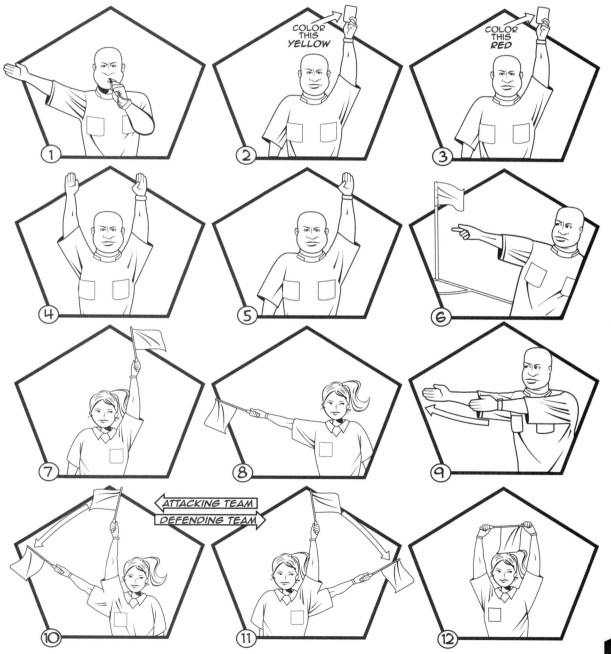

125

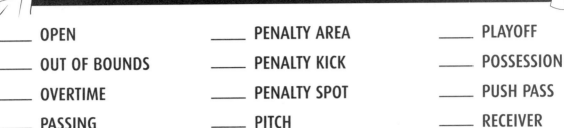

_____ OPEN   _____ PENALTY AREA   _____ PLAYOFF

_____ OUT OF BOUNDS   _____ PENALTY KICK   _____ POSSESSION

_____ OVERTIME   _____ PENALTY SPOT   _____ PUSH PASS

_____ PASSING   _____ PITCH   _____ RECEIVER

1. Describes a ball that goes past the touchline or goal line but not into the goal.

2. Soccer playing field.

3. A kick awarded for the most serious infractions committed by the defending team in their penalty area.

4. What a player is doing when they kick the ball to a teammate.

5. An extra period played when a game ends in a tie.

6. The rectangular area in front of the goal.

7. A tournament that follows the regular season to determine the champion.

8. The small circle in front of the center of the goal line from where all penalty kicks are taken.

9. A player who does not have anyone guarding them.

10. Control of the ball.

11. A kick to a teammate using the inside of one's foot.

12. The player who takes a pass from a teammate.

Grizzlies goalkeeper Garret moves up on Cougars forward Logan
to **cut his angle** on the goal, improving his chances of stopping Logan's shot.

131

____ RED CARD   ____ SHOULDER   ____ SHUTOUT

____ REFEREE   ____ SHIELD   ____ SIDELINE

____ RESTART   ____ SHORTHANDED   ____ SLIDE TACKLE

____ SAVE   ____ SHOT   ____ STADIUM

1. A team playing with fewer players than the opposing team.

2. A ball kicked or headed by a player toward the opposing team's net.

3. When a goalkeeper blocks or stops a ball from going into the net.

4. What takes place after a goal or infraction occurs.

5. When a team has at least one goal and prevents the opposing team from getting any goals.

6. Building where soccer is played.

7. The line that runs along the length of the pitch on both sides; also called the touchline.

8. A legal tackle where the player is low to the ground.

9. The head official on the field.

10. What a ball carrier does to protect the ball from an opposing player.

11. A legal tackle that a defender can make.

12. The card a referee holds up to indicate a player must leave the game.

CROSSWORD #3
SOCCER TERMS

ACROSS

WHEN THERE ARE NO DEFENDERS BETWEEN THE OPPOSING PLAYER AND GOALKEEPER

A GAME WHERE BOTH TEAMS END UP WITH THE SAME NUMBER OF GOALS

TWO PLAYERS SQUEEZE AN OPPOSING PLAYER AND STOP THEM FROM GETTING THE BALL

A TYPE OF KICK NAMED AFTER A FORM OF TRANSPORTATION

THE FIFTEEN MINUTES BETWEEN THE FIRST AND SECOND HALF OF A GAME

WHEN A PLAYER USES THEIR FEET TO CONTROL THE BALL

A TYPE OF RUN DESIGNED TO DISTRACT THE OPPOSING TEAM'S DEFENDERS

THE PART OF THE BODY A PLAYER IS NOT PERMITTED TO USE

DOWN

2. WHAT A PLAYER GAINS IF THEY LEAN ON A TEAMMATE WHILE TRYING TO SCORE

4. THE PASSES MADE TO THE PERSON WHO SCORES THE GOAL

5. WHEN A PLAYER GETS A BALL THAT WAS PASSED FROM ONE OPPOSING PLAYER TO ANOTHER

6. A METHOD OF DETERMINING A WINNER IF THE TEAMS ARE TIED AT THE END OF THE GAME

9. WHEN A PLAYER IS POSITIONED AHEAD OF BOTH THE BALL AND THE OPPOSING TEAM'S LAST DEFENDER

10. WHEN THE BALL IS KICKED BY A PLAYER BEFORE IT TOUCHES THE GROUND

11. A PLAYER BLOCKING AN OPPOSING PLAYER FROM GETTING TO THE BALL

15. A PASS THAT GOES OVER THE HEAD OF AN OPPOSING PLAYER

Eagles left fullback Dakota plays close to the edge of the pitch ensuring that Rebels forward Jade doesn't get a chance to attack from the right wing.

Rebels left fullback Amanda makes a **clean tackle**, taking the ball away from Eagles' forward Julie.

Grizzlies right center back Kyle moves the ball forward to begin his attack on the Cougars' goal.

———— 50/50 DRILL   ———— STRIKER   ———— THROUGH PASS

———— SLIDING TACKLE   ———— SUBSTITUTION   ———— THROW-IN

———— STARTER   ———— SWEEPER   ———— TOE KICK

———— STEAL   ———— THIGH TRAP   ———— TOUCHLINE

1. Take the ball away from an opposing player.

2. The replacement of one player on the field with another.

3. A type of restart taken by the team that did not kick the ball over the touchline.

4. An unreliable kick.

5. A player who is on the field at the start of the game.

6. The two longer lines that mark the edge of the pitch.

7. Use of the thigh to slow down and control the ball.

8. The forward who generally plays in the center and is often the team's best scorer.

9. A move in which a player slides on the ground in an attempt to take the ball away from an opposing player.

10. The fullback position considered the last defender, other than the goalkeeper.

11. A pass that goes between several defenders to a teammate.

12. Practice that teaches players to try and get to the ball before an opponent does.

GOOAALL!!!

Forwards, especially **strikers**, are usually strong goal scorers, as Eagles center forward Julie has shown. This was Julie's third goal of the game, giving her a **hat trick**.

Indirect attacking soccer makes use of sideways and backward
runs and passes while trying to find a weakness in the opposing team's
defense, in order to begin a forward attack.

143

When **defending to win,** all the players on the team push up to support the attack.

When **defending deep,** the fullbacks stay deep in their own half.

```
E S F E S B N N U U D C
A N G L E D I S F F O T
F U V D N A H R E V O I
N P E C I S C A R I T M
C E D E L I B E R A T E
R E I S H E A E C A V O
H O S C C N A K H A N U
C O T E U T L R S S P T
T I R E O E C L I E F S
P E A H T P E D A H O E
R E C E I V E L T C N O
I E T H A S E V O D H T
```

ANGLE

CLEAR

DELIBERATE

DEPTH

DISTRACT

OFFSIDE

ONSIDE

OVERHAND

PITCH

RECEIVE

SAVE

SPACE

TACKLE

TIMEOUT

TOUCHLINE

Cougars forward Tyler and midfielder Andrew create a **breakaway**. Grizzlies goalkeeper Garret will need to come up with a big save.

Spot the ten differences between pages 146 and 147.

 148

Eagles forward Taylor makes a **blind side run.**
She will be open to receive a pass from Eagles midfielder Asha.

Rebels forwards Jade and Lily make a **dummy run** to the right, distracting the Eagles defenders. This move creates space for Rebels midfielder Sarah to receive the pass from midfielder Louise.

The Eagles are playing **depth soccer**. They are concentrating their defense in a compact area between the ball and goal. If the Rebels break through, the Eagles are in a position to recover and stop the ball.

150

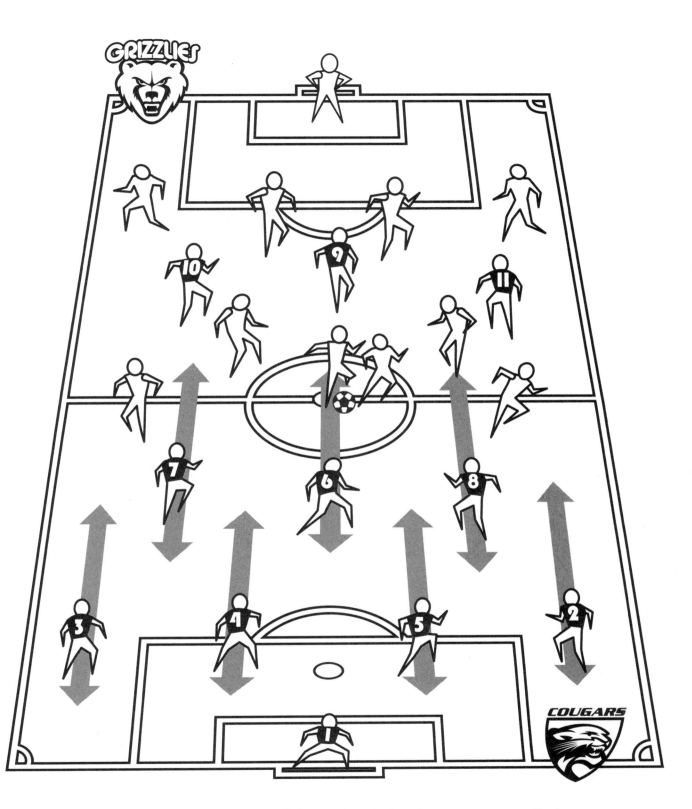

The Cougars move up and down the pitch using a strategy called
shift and sag which ensures that defensive layers are maintained.
They are concerned the Grizzlies might get a breakaway.

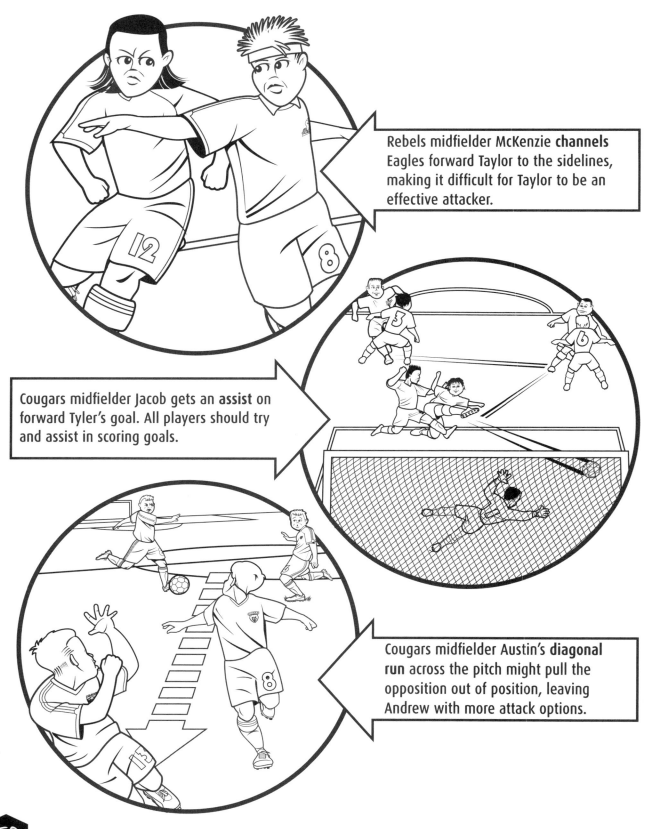

Rebels midfielder McKenzie **channels** Eagles forward Taylor to the sidelines, making it difficult for Taylor to be an effective attacker.

Cougars midfielder Jacob gets an **assist** on forward Tyler's goal. All players should try and assist in scoring goals.

Cougars midfielder Austin's **diagonal run** across the pitch might pull the opposition out of position, leaving Andrew with more attack options.

MATCH THE DESCRIPTION TO THE CORRECT SOCCER TERM #10

_____ SQUARE PASS   _____ TRAP   _____ WALL

_____ TIME-OUT   _____ TURNOVER   _____ WING

_____ TOUCHLINE   _____ UNSPORTSMANLIKE BEHAVIOR   _____ WORLD CUP

_____ TRAILING   _____ VOLLEY   _____ YELLOW CARDS

1. Loss of possession of the ball.

2. Lineup of defending players pressed shoulder to shoulder to protect their goal from a free kick.

3. A card the referee holds up to warn a player of dangerous or unsportsmanlike behavior.

4. An official break in play.

5. Running behind another player for a possible drop pass.

6. Poor behavior on the pitch.

7. An outside forward who plays closer to the touchline.

8. Use of the chest, thighs, or feet to slow down and control a ball.

9. The two lines that run down the sides of the pitch.

10. When a ball is kicked by a player off the ground.

11. An international soccer tournament held by FIFA every four years.

12. A pass that crosses the pitch at a ninety-degree angle.

Grizzlies midfielder Joel centers the ball with a **square pass** to open space in front of the Cougar goal. A square pass crosses the field at a ninety-degree angle.

Grizzlies fullback Lucas uses the **give-and-go strategy** to get himself and the ball past Cougars forward Conner.

155

Eagles forward Emma has open space to attack the Rebels' goal. Eagles midfielders Asha and Courtney created space. This is called **off-ball attacking**.

CONNECT THE DOTS

Rebels midfielder McKenzie creates space by dribbling the ball to
draw the Eagles' players toward her, freeing up her teammates to receive a pass.
This is called **on-ball attacking**.

157

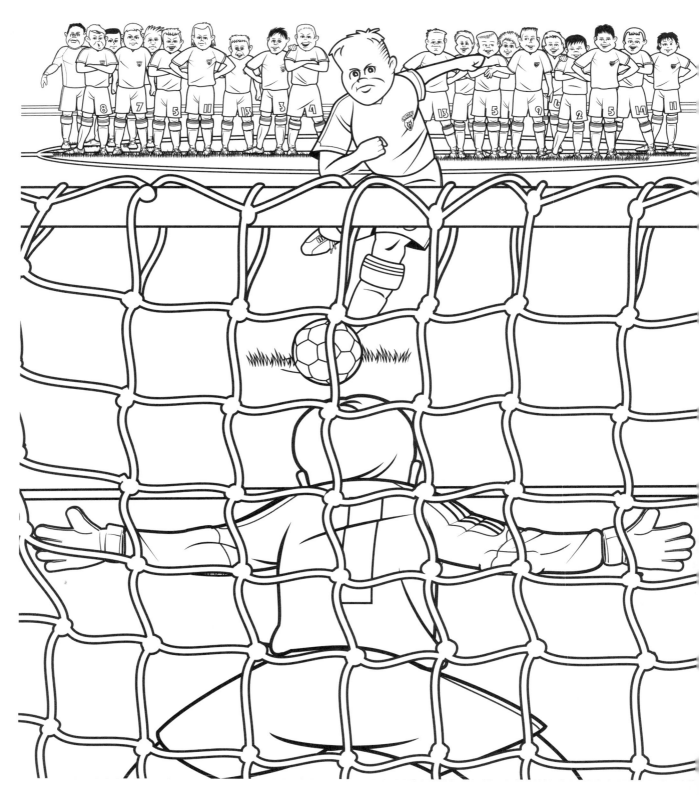

In a **shootout**, each team takes five kicks. If the teams score the same number of goals after five kicks, they continue until one team scores a goal and the other does not. All players must remain in the center circle during a shootout.

MAZE #4
SCORE A GOAL

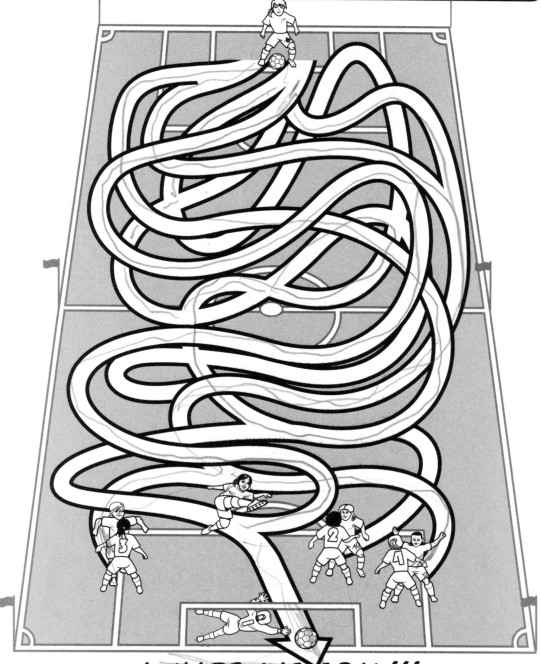

A-MAZE-ING GOAL!!!

Eagles midfielder Sofie needs to get the ball to Kara who is the only unmarked forward and is in position to score. Can you help her?

 It is important to show **good sportsmanship** regardless of which team wins or loses.

PUZZLE SOLUTIONS

MAZE SOLUTIONS

PAGE 21

PAGE 61

PAGE 124

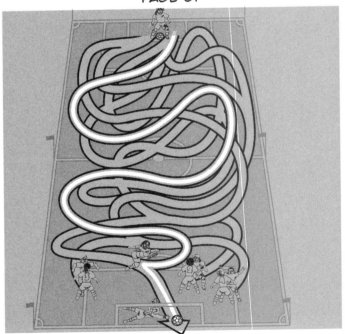

PAGE 159

SPOT THE DIFFERENCES SOLUTIONS

SPOT THE DIFFERENCES PAGES 40/41

SPOT THE DIFFERENCES PAGES 84/85

SPOT THE DIFFERENCES PAGES 102/103

SPOT THE DIFFERENCES PAGES 146/147

WORD MATCH SOLUTIONS

PAGE 25 GAME #1

8	ADVANTAGE CLAUSE RULE	3	BICYCLE KICK	10	CENTER SPOT
12	ASSIST	7	BREAKAWAY	9	CHEST TRAP
6	ATTACKING	2	CENTER BACK	1	CHIP PASS
11	BANANA KICK	4	CENTER CIRCLE	5	CHIP SHOT

PAGE 37 GAME #2

7	CHANNELS	9	CORNER KICK	3	CUT THE ANGLE
6	CLEAR THE BALL	12	CREATING SPACE	4	DEFENDERS
11	CORNER ARC	10	CROSSBAR	5	DEFENSIVE WALL
1	CORNER FLAG	2	CROSS PASS	8	DEFLECTION

PAGE 58 GAME #3

10	DIRECT FREE KICK	2	DRILL	1	FIFA
3	DIVE	11	DROP BALL	12	FLICK HEADER
8	DRAW	9	DROP KICK	7	FORMATIONS
5	DRIBBLE	6	FAKE	4	FOURTH OFFICIAL

PAGE 75 GAME #4

7	4-3-3	12	FRONT HEADER	9	GOALKEEPER
8	FIRST TOUCH	6	FULLBACKS	1	GOAL KICK
4	FORWARDS	11	GIVE-AND-GO	2	GOAL LINE
3	FOUL	5	GOAL AREA	10	HALFBACK

PAGE 87 GAME #5

4	HALFTIME	8	HOOK	5	IN-SWING PASS
2	HALF VOLLEY	7	IN BOUNDS	10	JUGGLING
12	HANDBALL	9	INDIRECT FREE KICK	3	KICKOFF
11	HAT TRICK	1	IN PLAY	6	LINESMEN

PAGE 118 GAME #6

11	LAWS OF THE GAME	7	MIDFIELD LINE	8	OFFENSIVE PLAYERS
1	LOFT	12	MLS	4	OFFICIALS
3	MAN ON	10	NET	9	OFFSIDE
5	MARK	2	NUTMEG	6	ONSIDE

PAGE 126 GAME #7

9	OPEN	6	PENALTY AREA	7	PLAYOFF
1	OUT OF BOUNDS	3	PENALTY KICK	10	POSSESSION
5	OVERTIME	8	PENALTY SPOT	11	PUSH PASS
4	PASSING	2	PITCH	12	RECEIVER

PAGE 132 GAME #8

12	RED CARD	10	SHIELD	5	SHUTOUT
9	REFEREE	1	SHORTHANDED	7	SIDELINE
4	RESTART	2	SHOT	8	SLIDE TACKLE
3	SAVE	11	SHOULDER	6	STADIUM

PAGE 137 GAME #9

12	50/50 DRILL	8	STRIKER	11	THROUGH PASS
9	SLIDING TACKLE	2	SUBSTITUTION	3	THROW-IN
5	STARTER	10	SWEEPER	4	TOE KICK
1	STEAL	7	THIGH TRAP	6	TOUCHLINE

PAGE 153 GAME #10

12	SQUARE PASS	8	TRAP	2	WALL
4	TIME-OUT	1	TURNOVER	7	WING
9	TOUCHLINE	6	UNSPORTSMANLIKE BEHAVIOR	11	WORLD CUP
5	TRAILING	10	VOLLEY	3	YELLOW CARDS

CROSSWORD PUZZLE SOLUTIONS

CROSSWORD #1 PAGE 27

CROSSWORD #2 PAGE 79

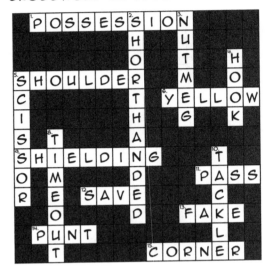

CROSSWORD #3 PAGE 133

WORD SCRAMBLE SOLUTIONS

WORD SCRAMBLE A–D, PAGE 68

PLAY ON AFTER FOUL	ADVANTAGE LAW
TO HELP	ASSIST
PLAYER WHO HAS BALL POSSESSION	ATTACKER
UPSIDE-DOWN KICK	BICYCLE KICK
TO GET AWAY	BREAKAWAY
PLAYER WHO LEADS THE TEAM ON THE PITCH	CAPTAIN
WHERE THE GAME STARTS	CENTER SPOT
RUN INTO ANOTHER PLAYER	CHARGE
WILL SLOW THE BALL	CHEST TRAP
PASS IN THE AIR	CHIP PASS
THEY GIVE SHOES TRACTION	CLEATS
AT THE CORNERS	CORNER ARC
TYPE OF RESTART	CORNER KICK
TOP PART OF GOALPOSTS	CROSSBAR
PLAYERS NOT IN POSSESSION OF THE BALL	DEFENDERS

WORD SCRAMBLE D–O, PAGE 100

CHANGE OF DIRECTION	DEFLECTION
MOVING THE BALL	DRIBBLING
TYPE OF RESTART	DROP BALL
TO FOOL	FAKE
UP FRONT	FORWARD LINE
GIVEN IF A FOUL OCCURS	FREE KICK
LAST DEFENDER	GOALKEEPER
TIME TO REST	HALFTIME
TOUCHING BALL WITH ILLEGAL BODYPART	HANDBALL
LET'S GET STARTED	KICKOFF
SENT AHEAD	LEAD PASS
THEY WATCH THE LINES	LINESMEN
STAY ON YOUR MARK	MAN-TO-MAN
WORKS THE MIDDLE	MIDFIELDER
IN CONTROL	OFFICIALS

WORD SCRAMBLE O–S, PAGE 113

OUT OF POSITION	OFFSIDE
IN THE CLEAR	OPEN
AFTER NINETY MINUTES	OVERTIME
MOVING THE BALL	PASSING
GOALKEEPER STOPS THE BALL	SAVE
TYPE OF SHOT	PENALTY SHOT
FIELD OF PLAY	PITCH
TO HAVE CONTROL OF THE BALL	POSSESSION
WAY OF MOVING THE BALL	PUSH PASS
PLAYER WHO GETS THE BALL	RECEIVER
REQUIRED TO LEAVE GAME	RED CARD
PITCH BOSS	REFEREE
GET A POINT	SCORE
PROTECTING THE BALL	SHIELDING
LEG PROTECTION	SHIN GUARD

WORD SCRAMBLE S–Z, PAGE 127

MISSING PLAYERS	SHORTHANDED
ONE TEAM DOESN'T SCORE	SHUTOUT
ATTEMPTING TO TAKE BALL	TACKLING
THEY PLAY FIRST	STARTER
KEY GOAL SCORER	STRIKER
REPLACEMENT	SUBSTITUTION
FULLBACK CLEANER	SWEEPER
TYPE OF RESTART	THROW-IN
A BREAK	TIME-OUT
SIDE OF PITCH	TOUCHLINE
LOSS OF POSSESSION	TURNOVER
BALL KICKED IN THE AIR	VOLLEY
AREA CLOSE TO SIDELINE	WING
WARNING	YELLOW CARD
FOOT MOVE TO KEEP THE BALL	SCISSOR MOVE

WORD SEARCH SOLUTIONS

PAGE 26

PAGE 26

WORD SEARCH
EQUIPMENT & FIELD REFERENCE

```
C A K C I Y E S R E J S
E R O S Y S N F G C A H
L O O G E L I E L R E I
T O B O L O L D L A U N
S C E A L L H A N R G G
I H U O C W S U A A N W A
H U O C W S U A A N W A
W T N S C W O N S R R R
A P E N A L T Y B O X D
T O P S R E T N E C N R
J E R E D C A R D D S G
C R O S S B A R H P O R
```

GAME #1

PAGE 60

PAGE 60

WORD SEARCH
SOCCER PERSONNEL

```
S W E E P E R F N A K R
C I O R E K I R T S E R
K S U B S T I T U T E C
C C W I N I A C R P N O
A D A I S C I A E A R A
B E I B K O T E M S R C
L F A E F S K S O M W H
L E R E D L E I F D I M
U N L E A N A A I M N E
F D E O I E E H E R G R
E E G L R E F E R E E M
D R A W R O F S A A R A
```

GAME #2

PAGE 119

PAGE 119

WORD SEARCH
PLAY TERMS

```
S P V O P A K N D B A
R K C I K R E N R O C
F I H F C V W E A D D
C C A S I I A P W L D
A K R D K K I O E F F
E O G O A L P O S T W
A F E W N J A F C S O
B F A A A S S I S T O
A Y C G N I L G G U J
R Y L L A B P O R D L
B A L A B F E N O K O
```

GAME #3

PAGE 145

PAGE 145

WORD SEARCH
STRATEGY

```
E S F E S B N N U U D C
A N G L E D I S F F O T
F U V D N A H R E V O I
N P E C I S C A R I T M
C E D E L I B E R A T E
R E I S H E A E C A V O
H O S C C N A K H A N U
C O T E U T L R S S P T
T I R A O E O E C L I E
P E A H T P E D A H O S
R E C E I V E L T C N O
I E T H A S E V O D H T
```

GAME #4

168

REFEREE SIGNAL GAME SOLUTIONS

PAGE 125

- (9) ADVANTAGE
- (2) CAUTION
- (6) CORNER KICK
- (1) DIRECT FREE KICK
- (10) FOUL BY ATTACKER
- (11) FOUL BY DEFENDER
- (4) GOAL
- (5) INDIRECT FREE KICK
- (7) OFFSIDE
- (3) SENDING OFF
- (12) SUBSTITUTION
- (8) THROW-IN

PAGE 157

IF YOU CONNECTED THE DOTS CAREFULLY, YOUR PAGE SHOULD LOOK LIKE THIS. IF NOT, DON'T WORRY. YOU CAN ALWAYS DRAW YOUR OWN ON THE NEXT PAGE.